Greetings From Tucson
A Postcard History of the Old Pueblo

By

Michelle B. Graye

Greetings From Tucson
Michelle B. Graye
2004

First edition 10 9 8 7 6 5 4 3 2 1

ISBN: 0-9760173-0-X

Printed in the United States of America
EBSCO Media

Michelle B. Graye
P.O. Box 1844
Tucson, AZ 85702

Cover design and scanning services by Daniel H. Caldwell
Copy editing by Shelby Meyer
Index by Michelle B. Graye

TABLE OF CONTENTS

ACKNOWLEDGMENTS

I would like to express my gratitude and appreciation to the following who have helped with my research and helped turn this book from a dream into a reality:

Arizona Historical Society, Tucson-Pima Public Library, Curt Teich Postcard Archives, Joan Gentry and the other post carders at the Tucson Post Card Exhange Club, The Laughin' Place, Esther Henderson, Bob Petley, Bunny Fontana, Bruce Dinges, Bonnie Henry, Tom Peterson, Shelby Meyer, Karen Thayer, Shari Graye, Joy Hartley, Liz Burden, and especially Daniel H. Caldwell for scanning all these postcards and his patience and guidance in keeping me from pulling my hair out by its roots.

A special thanks goes out to Clay Aiken for distracting me for about a year when I should have been working on this project.

I hope readers will enjoy *Greetings From Tucson*. This was truly a labor of love (well at least most days).

Michelle B. Graye
Author

INTRODUCTION

One of the defining moments in the history of Tucson was in 1695 when Padre Kino, a Jesuit missionary, entered the name "Tucson" on a map he had drawn. Tucson did certainly exist before this date. The area had been continuously inhabited for approximately 1,200 years when archaeologists unearthed a Hohokam pit house in the downtown area that dated the Hohokam presence somewhere between 700-900 A.D.

After Kino's naming of Tucson, it remained a small town for almost two hundred years; the population was 7,531 in 1900. Although growth was steady, it was not until the 1950s that Tucson started seeing a spectacular spurt in population owing to several factors:

- Following WWII, veterans were on the move, uprooting family and bringing them out West where many had trained and loved the warm desert climate.

- The invention of air conditioning, which allowed for the population to live in Tucson year round even during the sweltering heat of the summer.

The picture postcard debuted in the United States with the World's Columbian Exposition , held in Chicago in 1893, where the U.S. Post Office commissioned a set of cards to be sold at the fair which could be mailed at the two-cent letter rate. These postcards are historically important because the use of color photography was very rare. The average person could not afford to ever have color photographs taken, so black & white photos prevailed. Colorful postcards depicting famous U.S. landmarks started being issued mostly as souvenirs and mailed at the same rate for letters – 2 cents. The only space to write on these early postcards was a small space on the front of the card, hardly enough room to say "hello, how are you doing." This changed in 1907 when the divided back was born and travelers had a little more space to inquire about a relative's health and give a weather report, two of the most popular subjects talked about on the back of Tucson postcards.

One of the most popular postcards to send back to relatives was the so-called "Large Letter" greeting card which every city, town and state issued with the colorful mini-pictorials of the most well-known landmarks contained in each letter. Many recipients of postcards would hold onto them as keepsakes and these would result in a treasure trove for anyone wanting a glimpse back into the recent past. Every postcard used in this book is part of my own personal collection, with the majority of these being purchased through eBay. Though not a complete view of Tucson many places that have a fascinating history (i.e. Fourth Ave.) were not considered worthy subjects to put on postcards. *Greetings From Tucson* still manages to pull back the veil and give readers a snapshot history of Tucson not seen in the traditional histories written on the city.

One
WISH YOU WERE HERE

Luggage tag

The local Tucson Chamber of Commerce used this luggage tag/postcard as a marketing tool to reel in prospective visitors. Very clever on the Chamber's part to send these off in the month of December, when folks back in the East and Midwest were mired in miserable freezing weather. Former Mayor of Tucson Lew Murphy recalls his first trip to the Old Pueblo: "I had flown out from Minneapolis in December of 1950 for my Christmas holiday here with my family. And I left 40-degree-below-zero weather in Minneapolis, where you could freeze the rims off your ears by just going outdoors. And I got off in a sport coat at Tucson International Airport, and there was green grass. And it was hot."

Arizona Greetings map

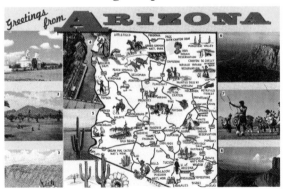

Arizona has always had a mystique as a place of natural beauty that offers up such exotic attractions as the Grand Canyon, cowboys and Indians, dude ranches, and even a meteor crater. At the beginning of the 20th century, Tucson boasted 7,531 inhabitants, making it the largest population center in the state. This trend held up until the 1920 census, when Phoenix counted 29,000 residents while Tucson had only 20,292. The booming metropolis of Phoenix has never looked back, with a current population of 1.3 million making it the sixth largest city in the United States.

Overview of Tucson

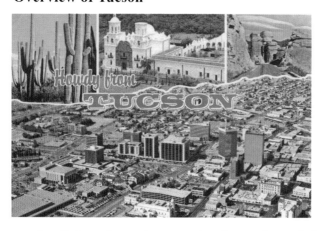

Pleasant climate has always been part of the charm of living in Tucson. The chamber of commerce never misses an opportunity to brag about the 3,800 hours of annual sunshine, which can be both a blessing and a curse, especially during the summer months. Various slogans incorporating the weather and charm of Tucson have been used over the years in promoting the "Old Pueblo," including "Home Beautiful City," "The Sunshine City of America," "Tucson Is a Way of Life," and "Tucson the Sunshine Factory."

Large Letter greeting card

One of the most popular postcards to send back to relatives was the so-called "Large Letter" greeting card which every city, town and state issued with the colorful mini-pictorials of the most well known landmarks contained in each letter. Many recipients of postcards would hold onto their postcards as keepsakes resulting in a treasure trove for anyone wanting a glimpse back into the recent past.

"A" Mountain

The Southern Pacific Hospital and Railroad are no longer located in this area, but in the railroad's heyday a thriving community supporting it, lived at the base of "A" Mountain. In the 1880s most of the workers on the railroad were Chinese, settling near the area below Sentinel Mountain and Tumamoc Hill.

The next big wave of immigrants, African Americans, moved to this community when a black developer built affordable housing for the minority veterans returning home from WWII.

Greetings from Tucson

A greetings postcard showing "A" Mountain, which was originally called Sentinel Peak. Before the frontier was really tame, a sentry would be posted atop the mountain to keep a vigilant watch and send danger signals if marauding Apache Indians were on the loose. Following a rousing victory for the U of A football team in the fall of 1915, some dedicated fans spent 14 consecutive Saturdays digging a trench on the mountainside facing the city and filling the trench with

rocks. Once completed, the rest of the student body joined in, forming a human chain, and passed up buckets of cement to pour around the rocks. White paint was then applied, and it's become a yearly tradition for the incoming freshman class to apply a fresh coat of paint every fall.

Large Letter greeting card

Another "Large Letter" greeting card, this one framed by a lovely senorita in the top left corner and the ubiquitous cactus on the bottom right. The heavily Spanish influence on Tucson's culture and architecture is very present on this card. Though the name Tucson (pronounced Too-sahn) sounds Spanish, it is Native American in origin. Tucson is from the Tohono O'odham word Tu-uk-so-on, or Chuk Shon, which refers to the black-stained volcanic rock at the base of Sentinel Peak (now known as "A" Mountain).

Tucson Souvenir Postcard Booklet

Picture postcards were often packaged as souvenir booklets and this served as a popular way to let the folks back home know all the highlights of your vacation.

What a charming way to communicate that seems to be lost in today's world where email in all of its impersonal glory has replaced the handwritten missive.

4

Convento

The convento, part of the original San Augstín del Tucson mission complex, was built at the base of what is now "A" Mountain. The convento, an important part of the Spanish presidio, was used to protect the citizens living on the

Ruins of Old Convent, built in 1776, Tucson, Arizona.

west side of the Santa Cruz River from Apache attacks. The convento had been standing proudly for almost 200 hundred years before falling into ruin and eventually disappearing by the 1950s. Recognizing the importance of this historical structure, the city excavated the original site and the convento will play an important part of the Rio Nuevo development plan to revitalize downtown Tucson.

Ft. Lowell Ruins

During the Civil War, the Union Army constructed a fort in downtown Tucson to protect the citizens from a possible attack by Confederate soldiers. In 1872 General George Crook called the encampment "unfit for the occupation of animals, much less the troops of a civilized nation" and moved Camp Lowell to a new post on the northeast part of town.

M68:—FORT LOWELL RUINS, NEAR TUCSON, ARIZONA

Michelle B. Graye

On my way to a good time

This postcard, showing a pot-bellied Mexican man sporting a Pancho Villa mustache and riding a burro, is using humor to not-so-subtly convey a stereotype about Mexicans that tourists might have. The stereotype revolves around their perceived lack of ambition and easy going demeanor and, of course, they only travel by burro wearing a ridiculous Mariachi outfit. The character is portrayed as harmless and somewhat of a buffoon but the card geared toward Anglo tourists is still a little unsettling.

The Trip's Been Uneventful...so far

Bob Petley has been using his considerable talents as an artist and photographer

to chronicle Tucson in postcards since 1945. This card is one of three black & white postcards he first issued in 1945. The genius of Petley is the whimsical way he is able to convey his message on such a small space. These black and white cards were sold from special three-sided racks trimmed with rope that were specially constructed for Bob. Petley cards are very collectible and a comprehensive checklist of his cards is a work in progress for the local Tucson postcard club.

Cartoon Card

This card was probably pretty risque for the time with the blatant sexual innuendo over the use of the word "ass" as a pun for the donkey as well as the woman's derriere. This would be an ideal postcard for the Mister to send

back home to his pals to let them know he's having a good time checking out the local scenery. The card plays to what every marketing campaign has known since the dawn of advertising, the power of sex to sell a product.

When Wind Blows in Tucson

This postcard seems to capitalize on the male tourist's fascination with Latina women which seems to play into the stereotype that they are exotic and loose with their morals. Worth noting on this card are the words in Spanish, "Que Buen Aire" which translates into, "What a nice breeze." No translation is provided, but I doubt that the men buying this card are using it to brush up on their Espanol.

Catalina Mountains

The majestic Santa Catalina Mountains are the most identifiable and most beloved mountain range in Tucson. It is a fairly uncommon sight to see the mountains so heavily covered with snow because the sun does a quick job of melting any snowfall in a matter of hours. The Santa Catalinas are referred to as

"sky islands," which means they are an isolated mountain chain that rises from the desert floor. The highest point of the Catalina Mountains is Mount Lemmon, rising to an elevation of 9,100 feet.

Bird's eye view at night

Showing a great view of what the Tucson skyline looks like at night, this photo was taken from "A" Mountain, one of the best vantage points from which to see the Tucson valley below. Fourth of July fireworks are held on "A" Mountain,

and residents for miles around can see the spectacular show from the comfort of their own backyards. Driving up to the top of "A" Mountain to see the city lights is popular with both the locals and visitors.

Two
GET YOUR FORTY WINKS HERE

El Encanto Estates

This postcard, published in 1940, shows one of the handsome homes situated in the exclusive El Encanto Estates. Located in central Tucson, the neighborhood show-cases some of the most beautiful homes that utilize several architectural styles including Period Revival. The neighborhood has 135 residences and El Encanto Estates is one of the few neighborhoods that can boast being on the Historic Register.

Michelle B. Graye

Harold Bell Wright home

253. HOME OF HAROLD BELL WRIGHT, NEAR TUCSON, ARIZONA.

Harold Bell Wright was a wildly popular author in the early 20th century and his books including his most well-known *The Mine with the Iron Door*, have sold over 10 million copies between the years 1903 and 1942. Wright moved permanently to Tucson in 1919 to regain his health after his tuberculosis flared up. He thought the slower pace of Tucson and the natural beauty of the Southwest would be a positive influence on his writing. Wright found an isolated piece of property on the outskirts of town to build a desert home to his specifications. In Wright's world the perfect place would have to incorporate "his love of the desert, his dislike of gaping tourists, his appreciation of Indian architecture, and his own comfort while writing."

Typical desert home

This postcard shows the typical home for the average Tucson resident. Building with adobe and clay tile roofs is a popular choice for construction of homes.

Typical Desert Home, Spanish Type, Tucson, Arizona.

Since water is such a scarce commodity, the homeowner usually embraces desert landscaping which is out in full force in this postcard. Note the gorgeous mountain view which serves as the backdrop for this home.

Steinfeld residence

Located on North Main, this brick and stucco house built in 1902 was designed by renowned local architect Henry Trost. Once home to the Owl's Club, a local gentleman's club, the structure is now known as the Steinfeld House. The mansion has been restored and is now used for offices. This home lays claim to one of the first houses to have bathtubs and piped in running water. This house is a great example of the California Mission Revival-style of architecture dating from 1900.

The "Steinfeld Residence",
North Main St., Tucson, Ariz.

Manning mansion

Named after Levi Howell Manning, a turn-of-the century merchant, developer and politician who built this 10,000 square feet mansion around the time he was entering office as Tucson mayor in 1905. Constructed for just around $10,000, this house features a blend of Spanish Colonial and Santa Fe Territorial architecture styles. The mansion is located in "Snob Hollow" where many of Tucson's movers and shakers lived in the 1900s.

Col. Manning's Residence, Tucson, Arizona.

Just around the corner from Colonel Manning's mansion was a high priced whore house called "Mary's house." Prostitution was legal in Tucson in the early 1900s and this red-light district house never lacked for business. The girls got regular health check-ups to keep in good standing with their gentlemen callers.

Santa Rita Hotel

Colonel Manning built this hotel in 1904 as a response to a complaint by a tourist about the bed bugs at the other local hotels. In its heyday the magnificent Santa Rita Hotel was a favorite hangout for the well-heeled out-of-towners, movie stars

and cattlemen with its distinctively Western flavor. The manager, Nick Hall, was a bit of a curmudgeon who favored cow-boys, cowgirls and ranchers over the usual businessman types who came to town. Some of the big name guests that came for stays at the Santa Rita Hotel include Clark Gable, Jimmy Stewart, John Wayne, Helen Hayes, Errol Flynn, Louis Armstrong and Paul Newman. Gregory Peck made quite an impression on some of the guests when he rode his horse through the lobby after a day of shooting *Duel in the Sun*.

Santa Rita Hotel ballroom

The ballroom was a swinging place and some of the legendary big bands that played at the Santa Rita Hotel include Benny Goodman, Artie Shaw, and Glenn

Miller who actually commanded $1,000 a night for perform-ing. The ballroom was really fancy with its art deco decor, and until its demise in 1972 was one of the great hotels in Tucson's history.

El Conquistador Hotel

Other than the downtown area, Tucson did not have much in the way of resort hotels for the visiting tourists. In the 1920s with the help of Colonel Manning, the Tucson Chamber of Commerce put together a bold plan to build a resort hotel to appeal to well-heeled travelers from out of town. Selling stock in the future resort, the committee raised $300,000 and hired noted architect Henry O. Jaasted to design the hotel. In 1928 with construction delays and escalating costs, Jaasted dropped out and developer John Murphey ended up completing

the project. Open for business on November 22, 1928 the El Conquistador was the ultimate in swanky living, offering guests ballroom dancing, fancy dining, golfing and even a riding stable.

El Con Mall

Once the El Conquistador was no longer a big money producing entity, the building was torn down in the name of progress. Pieces of the El Conquistador are still spotted in Tucson, including the copper dome now located at the Casa Blanca Shopping Center as well as part of the original facade which serves as the entrance to the Sin Vacas gated community. A new concept in shopping was the wave of the future in America and that was the enclosed mall. Americans in the 1950s were discovering a new concept in retail shopping – convenience. The El Con Mall opened in the late

1960s and was the first enclosed mall in Tucson. The El Con Mall has been often blamed as being the chief culprit for the decay of Tucson's downtown.

Michelle B. Graye

Arizona Inn

The Arizona Inn, one of Tucson's most beautiful and well recognized hotels, got its start in a very unusual manner. Following WWI, Isabella Greenway, a com-

munity leader and Arizona's first female member of Congress, was hiring disabled veterans and turning them into craftsmen at her furniture factory, the Arizona Hut. With the stock market crash of 1929 and the Great Depression that followed, Greenway lost some of her lucrative contracts. But, instead of closing up her factory, she built an inn to house all the fine furniture created by her workers. The rest, is as they say, history and the Arizona Inn is a thriving entity known for its charm and beautiful decor both inside and out.

Lodge on the Desert

The Lodge on the Desert was originally designed as a private residence in 1931, then sold to a married couple, Cornelia and Homer Lininger. The Liningers opened for business as a guest lodge with seven rooms in 1936, convinced that

travelers would embrace year around stays at their quaint lodge even during off season. A swimming pool and corral, which are still in use today, were the last touches added to the Lodge.

Major Motel

To satisfy the needs of the traveling public for an inexpensive but clean place to stay, the auto courts were born. Tucson was such a convenient city to drive through, even if stays were short, so dotting a stretch on Highway 80 were

dozens of these tourist courts. Most of these auto courts were mom-and-pop operations that provided cabins that were really small, usually around 200 square feet, and sometimes guests were even expected to supply their own curtains and sheets. A popular feature to advertise was "air cooled" which does not mean air conditioning for the uninitiated into the charms of evaporative cooling.

Don Motel

The Don Motel is an example of how a typical auto court (the word motel had not entered the lexicon yet), was set up with the stand alone buildings having parking located between the units. By the 1930s, the number of cars pursuing the American dream of unlimited open road had skyrocketed, and auto courts, or tourist courts, were having their salad days. Over time, these courts would evolve into motels, and slowly their market share dwindled, having to share with the low budget motel chains sprouting up like weeds in the 1950s and 1960s.

Sun-Ray Motel

The Sun-Ray Motel makes the most of flaunting the appeal of all that Arizona sunshine by using a sun motif on their postcard. Got to wonder about the sun

bathing patio featured very prominently on this postcard. I can't image the average tourist would find it appealing hanging outside in 100 degree heat and sun worshipping at a brick wall. The Sun-Ray Motel is still in operation today.

El Rancho Motor Hotel

The El Rancho Motel with their generic sounding Spanish name seems to be aiming towards the tourist that wants a little south of the border flavor. Their motto

trumpets "For people who live well" and, if you can handle cracker box dimensions, that shouldn't be a problem at the El Rancho Motor Hotel. Using the modern name "motor hotel" versus "auto court," the rooms now are under one roof instead of separate units.

Flamingo Hotel

Conveniently located on Stone Avenue near downtown Tucson, the Flamingo Hotel has seen its glory days come and go. Trying to capture some of that glitz and glamour of its Las Vegas namesake, the Tucson Flamingo Hotel was a happening place for film crews working on movies at Old Tucson in the 1950s. Besides being a hotel, the Flamingo has wall-to-wall Western movie-themed posters and other movie memorabilia. Certainly not a four star hotel, but the kitsch and the retro fifties look of the hotel make this one shag-a-licious place to stay.

El Presidio Hotel

The El Presidio, located in the historic district of downtown, offered up such amenities as a pool, solarium and the Silver Spur bar where visitors could enjoy nightly cocktails. The hotel ran into problems in 1978 when it was deemed not to be up to fire code and had to close its top three floors.

Three
YOU CAN ALWAYS GO DOWNTOWN

The lights are much brighter there
You can forget all your troubles,
forget all your cares, so go downtown.

Petula Clark – *Downtown*

Bird's-eye view of Tucson

Downtown Tucson, though not a huge megalopolis, still offered up a nice com-pact space perfect for a population that lived and worked downtown in the early 1900s through the 1950s. Downtown Tucson today is fairly busy during the

week with government and office workers, but it virtually empties out once 5:00 p.m. hits when the office work-ers head home. Efforts are currently underway with a Rio Nuevo proj-ect to revitalize the downtown with a care-fully thought out plan and an infusion of gov-ernment and private money to bring back some of that "traffic in the city" that Petula Clark so eloquently sings about in her classic song *Downtown*.

Downtown postcard booklet

It's hard to believe that in the recent past downtown was the place to shop and

socialize and served as the social center of Tucson. Marjorie Manning, a pro-minent socialite, called it "an old cow town. Everybody knew every-body. You couldn't go downtown and get any-thing done because you would stop on the street and visit with someone you know."

18

Bird's-eye view of downtown

The downtown area was always seen as the hub, even when the Spanish used it as a presidio and walled up the city to serve as a fort. By 1877 Tucson had two hotels, a county court-house, a United States depository, two brew-eries, two flour mills, four livery stables and ten saloons. Tucson even had running water, a luxury for those days.

Bird's Eye View of Tucson, Ariz.

More modern bird's-eye view

This postcard shows an overhead view of the downtown area with the Pima County Courthouse which serves as the centerpiece in modern downtown Tucson. A mix of contemporary and old world architec-ture blend in to make downtown Tucson a charming place for tourists and residents alike.

TUCSON, ARIZONA

19

Barrio district

2397. A STREET IN OLD TOWN. TUCSON, ARIZ.

This postcard shows some of the historic Barrio district which at one time was an eclectic mix of adobe homes, old hotels, cafes, saloons, houses of prostitution and populated mostly by Hispanic Americans. Many of the barrio homes were built in the 1870s and the typical home had no front yard, with the house facing an alley where a rear courtyard could be added on as needed. Not everyone valued the historic value of these old adobe homes, and during the 1960s the City Council approved the decision to level over 200 adobe structures to make way for La Placita Village and the Tucson Community Center.

Washington Park

The original name for this site was Military Plaza which became Camp Tucson

Washington Park, Tucson, Ariz.

after the California Column established an encampment here in 1862. The name game continued with Camp Tucson becoming Camp Lowell and eventually moved from downtown to its present site now called Ft. Lowell. In 1900 land was set aside on the Military Plaza for the Carnegie Free Library and a city park. The city still wasn't done tinkering with names and Washington Park became Armory Park in 1914 after construction of the armory.

Congress Street showing trolley

In 1879 Tucson used the mule-drawn carriage as their major form of public transportation. This inefficient and always complained about transit system was replaced by a street railway line in 1898. The "streetcars" were still drawn by mules and horses causing lots of delays in getting to your destination when the horses would lie down in the middle of the streets. In June 1906 the mule-drawn car made its

Congress Street, Tucson, Ariz

last run in Tucson, replaced by an electric trolley car nicknamed "The Izzer." The trolley finally stopped service in 1930 replaced by a bus system which was more efficient but lacked the character of "The Izzer."

Congress Street

Congress was very heavily used by automobiles and was always a lively street that can lay claim to many firsts including first traffic light (installed on March 14, 1927 at the corner of Congress & Sixth Ave.), first water main, first school building (1876 on Congress between Scott & Sixth Ave), and first dime store (Kress, opening its doors in 1876).

Michelle B. Graye

Congress Street Looking West

Another view of Congress Street looking west. Congress was the hub of shopping activity with some stores that are very familiar to long-time Tucsonans. The Levy's Department Store was opened in 1903 in Douglas and even had Pancho Villa, the revolutionary general, as a customer. The Martin Drug Company was part of a chain of eight drugstores and has the distinction of being the first drugstore in the territory to have a soda fountain.

Congress Street in the 1950s

A more modern view of Congress Street, looking west, and the timeframe is the 1950s when downtown Tucson was enjoying the last throes of being the focal point for shopping and commerce. Notice how nice everyone dressed to come downtown. The downtown had three drugstores with McClelland's being one of the most popular with teenagers. An easy bus ride downtown, the youngsters could listen to 45 rpm records and enjoy a soda at the counter with pocket change stretching far enough to buy all kinds of cool five & dime items.

Fox Theatre on Congress Street

The Fox Theatre shown in this postcard was an ornately designed movie palace that had its glory days between 1920 and 1945. When originally built, the Fox

was designed for vaudeville and silent movies and had a Wurlitzer organ for the occasional live performance. The Mickey Mouse Club was a mainstay on Saturday mornings and all the seats were filled. Sadly, the Fox closed its doors in 1974 and, with the renewed interest in reviving downtown, the Fox has been undergoing extensive renovations and will in the near future be once again back in business acting as a magnet to draw crowds to visit downtown.

Congress Street at night

Congress Street has always been considered one of the main thoroughfares for Tucson for nearly two centuries. Located on Congress Street were such diverse

businesses and shops as the Fox Theatre, El Frente Azul (The Blue Front) mercantile store, the Recreation saloon, the Opera House (where Sarah Bernhardt performed with her five carloads of costumes, scenery and props), Kress Drugstore, two cafes, and a bank.

23

Stone Avenue early view

Despite being a main thoroughfare of travel, Stone Avenue did not get paved until 1911. The unpaved road made life miserable for travelers because huge dust clouds would blow up when cars moved from intersection to intersection until the water wagons came in with sprinkling equipment. The poles shown on the left in this postcard were for telephone wires, and the ones on the right were for electric power.

Stone Avenue at night

A night scene of the Tucson shopping district which is highlighted by the neon Steinfeld's sign with the Conestoga wagon that would actually appear to be moving. The Steinfeld's Department Store was a joint venture between Albert

Steinfeld and his uncles, William & Lewis Zeckendorf, who had opened the first department store in Tucson in 1869 called Zeckendorf & Company.

24

Pioneer Hotel

The Pioneer Hotel was one of the most popular hotels right in the heart of downtown Tucson. The hotel, built in 1929, was one of the city's first skyscrapers and ranked up there as one of the most popular hotels for businessmen and tourists to come for a stay. During World War II, the hotel was a hangout for the soldiers training in Tucson and, after a hard day on the base, soldiers could get really amorous in the basement "passion pit" on very busy dance nights.

T-24   Stone Avenue Looking South, Tucson, Arizona

Skyscrapers on Stone Avenue

Tucson's first two skyscrapers (built in 1929) look quite majestic in this linen postcard. The Pioneer Hotel and the Valley National Bank (originally called Consolidated National Bank) were built around the same time and were the dual centerpieces in Tucson's attempt to remake its image from sleepy cow town to sophisticated big city.

The early hotels and resorts catered primarily to Hollywood actors and big name politicians who arrived with staff, servants, and steamer trunks to take up residence mostly in the winter months in Tucson.

25

Four
BUILD IT AND THEY WILL COME

Pima County Courthouse with mountain view

One weekend each October the ever popular "Tucson Meet Yourself" festival

Pima County Court House, Tucson, Arizona. Santa Catalina Mountains in background— Portion of Old City of Tucson wall in foreground

takes place on the Presidio Park on the west side of the courthouse giving downtown visitors an opportunity to bask in the shadow of this gorgeous building while enjoying an authentic sampling of various ethnic foods.

City Hall

Now long gone, Tucson's City Hall seemed cursed from its initial construction in April 1916 with the mayor loudly complaining about the shoddy beams supporting the roof. The first architect was called away for National Guard duty leaving the project to be finished by a new architect who urged the City Council to jettison the entire project because of the poor design. The hapless architect was ordered to finish the job and when finally completed in early 1917, City Hall served multiple functions including a basement jail that housed the drunk tank,

City Hall.   Tucson, Arizona.

an unpleasant place for staff to work with the overcrowded conditions and sometimes smelly prisoners. The City Hall stood for over fifty years and finally had a date with the wrecking ball and was demolished in 1972.

Scottish Rite Cathedral

The Scottish Rite Cathedral, also known as the Masonic Temple, was the brain-child of George J. Roskruge who came to Arizona in the 1870s. A Mason himself, Uncle George (as he was affectionately called) founded the first Masonic lodge in Prescott.

Once Roskruge moved to Tucson he proved to be a popular civic leader and quickly got the support of the local Masons to get the Cathedral built. The first cornerstone for the building was laid in 1915. The building is still an active lodge serving more than 3,000 members.

First Baptist Church

The First Baptist Church understood the power of promoting church services and

used this postcard to let members know of any special activities or events worth attending. Reverend Beal, a local firebrand, was instrumental in seeing this church built and on Easter Sunday in 1926 the church had its grand opening.

Michelle B. Graye

Catholic Cathedral

The Saint Augustíne Cathedral, located on Stone Avenue, was the second Catholic church established in Tucson. Built in the Romanesque Revival style, this church even though constructed of brick-clad iron columns suffered a collapse of the iron pipes inside during its construction. The "French" style of archi-

tecture was not considered appropriate for Spanish and Mexican parishioners, so a major remodeling of the church was ordered. See the postcard below for the incredible makeover this cathedral underwent in the late 1920s

Saint Augustíne Cathedral

Originally called San Augustín Cathedral (the first one built in 1863 is in a different location) is now known as the Saint Augustíne Cathedral. A major remod-

eling was undertaken in the 1920s completing the truncated towers, adding a spectacular facade in the Spanish Colonial Revival Style. A bronze statue of St. Augustine stands watch above the doorway.

Benedictine Sanctuary

The Benedictine monastery was built in 1940 by Roy and Lew Place, a father and son architecture team, for the Benedictine sisters who first came to Tucson in 1935. The sisters first lived in the Steinfeld mansion until the monastery was completed. The Spanish Colonial Mission style building has 39 bedrooms and a chapel and is a working monastery for the nuns who live there. To support their mission, the nuns bake unleavened bread and sell the loaves to other Catholic Churches around the world.

American Legion Building

The state of Arizona was granted one of the first charters by the American Legion to have a building honoring their veterans. It took almost 20 years for the local vets to raise enough funds to put a building on the designated site. The building is named to honor Morgan McDermott, a young World War I soldier, who was killed in action shortly before the signing of the armistice treaty.

St. Philip's in the Hills

The St. Philip's in the Hills Episcopal Church was designed to anchor the

Catalina Foothills Estates project of John Murphey, a local developer. Built in 1936, this elegant church is a great example of the Spanish Colonial Revival style. The Church had some changes in 1957 and 1998 with additions added on. Though not one of Tucson's older buildings, St. Philip's has a rustic, intimate feel enhanced by the gorgeous view of the Santa Catalina Mountains.

.

Mission in the Sun

Well loved and respected local artist Ted De Grazia hand-built this mission

in 1950 to honor Father Kino. The Mission in the Sun has thick adobe walls with a unique design that features murals of angels on the interior walls and a small shrine dedicated to Our Lady of Guadalupe in the back of the tiny chapel. Located on the same property as the Gallery in the Sun, visitors with an appreciation for De Grazia's artistry have made this a must see stop when visiting Tucson.

VA Hospital

With the dry desert heat and almost year around sunshine, Tucson had a reputation as a healing center drawing in thousands of soldiers who had been victims of mustard gassing during World War I. Suffering from tuberculosis, their cure of the day was lots of sunshine and rest. The soldiers lived outside on cots in what was called Tent City. Eventually the veterans became organized and campaigned for a real hospital. In 1929 the

Veterans Hospital opened and the building is a perfect example of the Spanish Colonial Revival style. Designed by Roy Place, the pink stucco buildings are recognizable by anyone driving down South 6th Avenue and the hospital still functions as a place where ill veterans can receive medical care.

St. Mary's Hospital

To understand the history of St. Mary's Hospital you have to just follow the remarkable trail of the Seven Sisters of St. Joseph of Carondelet who made the month-long trek in their heavy black habits from Missouri to Tucson, their mission to open an Indian school. Their work on the trade school was postponed because, with the arrival of the Southern Pacific Railroad, a hospital seemed a more pressing priority. With the help of

Bishop Salpointe and Tohono O'odham workers, it took a year of hard labor which paid off for the sisters when the 12-bed hospital was completed in 1880. St. Mary's was the first hospital in the Arizona territory.

Michelle B. Graye

Carnegie Free Library

Any city that wants to be considered great has to have a library to offer its citizenry an opportunity to enrich their lives through the power of reading. Well

known philanthropist Andrew Carnegie was offering land and money to cities across America to build public libraries. In 1883, Tucson only had a small library that was operating out of city hall so the library board jumped at the chance when Carnegie offered up $25,000 and land to build a free standing library. Architect Henry Trost won the design competition and chose to build the Carnegie Free Library in Neoclassical Revival style.

Carnegie Free Library

The Carnegie Free Library opened for business in 1901 and this handsome building illustrates some of the finest craftsmanship of the day with the Ionic tow-

ers, central dome, buff-colored bricks and plaster ornamentation. The building has held up to many design changes over the years including a massive wall enclosing the front of the library and a 1941 fire that destroyed the central dome. The Tucson Public Library moved to new quarters on Stone Avenue in 1990, leaving this building for its new incarnation as the Tucson Children's Museum.

Pima County Courthouse side view

Considered by many to be the most beautiful building after the San Xavier Mission, the Pima County Courthouse designed by Roy Place is always a welcome sight for anyone coming downtown. This is the third courthouse with the second one being condemned in 1927 when a huge crack appeared along its south wall and the second floor started to sag. The citizens of Tucson approved a huge bond of

$300,000 to build the courthouse but some questioned the heavily Spanish flavor of the architecture as inappropriate for a government building.

Pima County Courthouse front view

In 1929, when first opened, the courthouse was located in the heart of downtown and housed everyone from the county school superintendent to the Sheriff's office and even prisoners.

CONSOLIDATED NATIONAL BANK BUILDING. TUCSON, ARIZONA

Consolidated National Bank

The Consolidated National Bank Building has the distinction of being one of Tucson's first skyscrapers, built in just over a year at a total cost of one million dollars. 1929 was not the best year to be building banks the stock market had its crash just 10 days after the bank opened its doors. Once billed as the most beautiful in the Southwest, this bank has been featured in several movies, including the 1956 film noir *A Kiss Before Dying* in which Robert Wagner tried to push a woman off the top of the building and *Stir Crazy*, the 1980 buddy movie starring Richard Pryor and Gene Wilder playing inept bank robbers.

Pioneer Hotel

The Pioneer Hotel was the location of one of the most tragic fires in Tucson's history. On December 19, 1970, a Christmas party in the ballroom was still going strong around midnight. Two floors above, Lewis Taylor, a sixteen-year-old boy with a juvenile record, set the building on fire. The flames and smoke really started spread-ing fast, engulfing the twelve story building, and 28 peo-ple perished (includ-ing Peggy and Harold Steinfeld). Lewis Taylor was arrested and convict-ed for the crime and sentenced to life in prison.

Post Office and Federal Building

The Post Office and Federal Building, designed by James A. Wetmore in Neoclassical style, was built in 1929. The original configuration had a ground-floor post office with court rooms occupying the second floor. With the arrival of the railroad, building materials from both East and West coasts were easily available for the first time, hence this building really strays from the popular

Post Office and Federal Building, Tucson, Arizona

Spanish/Southwestern adobe flavor so dominant in the downtown. This Federal Building is still standing today waiting for its next incarnation as part of the Rio Nuevo redevelopment plan for downtown Tucson.

Old Pueblo Club

The Old Pueblo Club, founded in 1907 as a "gentleman's club," was an early example of the importance of schmoozing with your fellow elite leaders and high echelon businessmen. The city's top wheelers and dealers would meet regularly to socialize and conduct formal business. Such noted celebrities as Charles Lindbergh, "Buffalo Bill" Cody, John Wayne, Theodore

New Bldg. of the "Old Pueblo Club", Tucson, Ariz.

Roosevelt, and William Howard Taft were guests of the club.

Original Train Depot

This postcard shows the 2nd train depot built at the site of the original Southern Pacific Railroad station. The much anticipated arrival of the Southern Pacific Railroad in 1880 prompted a presidential visit from Rutherford B. Hayes. In 1880 the mayor of Tucson was so excited about the train that he wrote to the

Pope in Rome claiming Tucson was now connected to the Christian world. Some jokester friends of the mayor sent a fake telegram back: "Congratulations, but where the hell is Tucson?" It was in this railroad yard near the station where, in March 1882, Wyatt Earp killed Frank Stillwell to avenge the murder of his brother Morgan. Once the railroad station moved to a new location, the building has been used for other purposes and is currently a Mexican restaurant called Garcia's.

Southern Pacific Railroad Depot

The Southern Pacific Railroad is currently housed at this location. Most early travelers to Tucson arrived at this building before being shuttled off to their real

destination. During the depression people would be traveling on top of boxcars. During the great flu epidemic, trains were always late because of the time it took to unload the corpses. The first automobile that came to Tucson arrived at this depot. In 1905, when Dr. Fenner's car arrived to great fanfare, he took it around for a spin and promptly ran it into a saguaro, so he gets tagged with having the first auto accident in Tucson's history as well.

Temple of Music and Art

Built in 1927, the Temple of Music and Art was the first community-organized theatrical and cultural arts center. Madeleine Heineman, a local music teacher, organized her friends to put on weekly music lessons and concerts. It was largely through Madeleine's efforts that the Temple of Music and Art became such an important cultural center. The building is very reminiscent of the Pasadena Community Playhouse and it's no surprise the architect Arthur W. Hawes did assist in the design of the Playhouse. With $200,000 raised from community members, construction on this Spanish Colonial Revival-style building began in 1927.

268 TEMPLE OF MUSIC AND ART, TUCSON, ARIZONA   119766

Tucson High School

Built for $75,000, this Neoclassic style building opened for students in 1924. Well-known alumni include Floyd Thompson (Tucson's first black dentist), Apollo 8 astronaut Frank Borman, and pop singer Linda Ronstadt. Tucson High had a reputation as being the best school in Tucson, with a melting pot of races attending. Hispanic students were not allowed to speak Spanish on the school grounds however, which did cause some dissent among the more enlightened teachers.

Tucson Senior High School, Tucson, Arizona   322

Five
YEE-HAW! COWBOYS & INDIANS

Ole Southwest

The Old West conjures up the most fanciful images in the minds of people who don't actually live there. Thanks to countless movies and television shows, and even before that radio westerns and dime store novels, there was an undeniable romance about anything associated with cowboys and Indians. Tourists loved to send postcards back home that portrayed Tucson as still stuck in frontier days.

Group of Tucson Indians

Native Americans have always lived where Tucson stands, and the sixteen

different tribes in Arizona make it the state with the highest Native American population. Cowboys and Indians are as much a part of Tucson's heritage as frijoles and fiesta.

Cowboy roping a steer

A cowboy trying to toss his lariat over a young steer show-cases one of the many skills a cow-boy needs to be suc-cessful at his trade. Chasing down a run-away dogie while on the back of a speed-ing horse would have to qualify as one of the original extreme sports. Kids looking at this postcard, don't try this at home now with the family pet.

Winter rodeo

Tucson not only hosts the big Fiesta de los Vaqueros but sponsors other rodeo events as well. The rodeo roper shown in this photograph was probably not the only black man on the circuit, considering African American men have a strong tradition as cowboys on the frontier. African Americans were on cattle drives, fought Indians, broke wild horses, served as lawmen, and were an important force in taming the frontier. Participat-ing in the rodeo was often a natural extension of their skills honed as cowboys.

Way Out West

Tucson as a podunk town where nothing happens was probably a particularly appealing joke to the city slicker tourists from the big cities in the Midwest and East. If cowboys weren't getting lickered up and shooting up the town what else

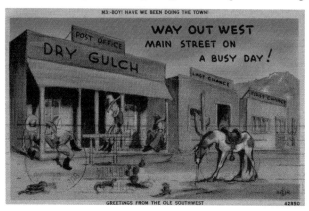

was there to do but catch some zzzzzs between all the hell-raising. For the record Tucson is located way out in the Southwest not the West, but that's another story.

Horseback riding at Tanque Verde Ranch

In the 1920s, James Converse, who owned the Tanque Verde ranch at the time, allowed occasional paying guests to stay for short one-or two-week visits. This concept soon proved popular and was copied by other working ranches through-

out Tucson and Southern Arizona. Stunning mountain views, lots of fresh air and the opportunity to stay at a dude ranch spawned a whole new tourist industry for Tucson starting in the 1920s when once profitable cattle ranches started to decline.

Lady in chaps

You don't think that sex sells postcards? This little gem was probably a favorite with the male of the species and the young whipper-snapper cowboys have to do something to keep themselves occupied while lollygagging

outside the general store. Artists always take an easy shortcut to place the geographic locale in Tucson by including a cactus somewhere on the postcard.

Bare-back riding cartoon postcard

This was considered a racy postcard for its time. It's nice to know that dumb blonde jokes were even the fashion back in the 1950s when this card was popular, a postcard obviously geared toward the guys, having an attractive blonde babe riding her horse in Lady Godiva fashion. The attentive cowboys are trying to be helpful but notice they aren't being very gallant about taking off their shirts and offering some protection for this clueless lassie.

41

Michelle B. Graye

Chuck wagon

Chuck Wagon of The Ole Southwest

Plenty of Meat, Potatoes, Frijoles and Coffee about to be consumed

This postcard depicts a chuck wagon outing with the cowboys. The main staples of food were cooked beef, potatoes, frijoles (beans), and coffee. Back when cowboys participated in the great trail drive, the men had to make do with what they could carry with them. Charles Goodnight, a Texas rancher, came up with a workable solution to this problem and in 1866 he took an army surplus Studebaker wagon and created the prototype for the chuck wagon.

Wild Horse Ranch chuck wagon

The dude ranch version of a chuck wagon for guests wanting a taste of the cowboy life. The postcard is from the Wild Horse Ranch, a twenty-acre ranch that originally started as a mining camp and attracted movie star clientele such as Jimmy Stewart and Paul Newman.

Branding calves

Arizona ranch woman Florence Meyer recalls how her husband couldn't make a go of cattle ranching in the late 1920s, which led to the formation of their working dude ranch: "[My husband] went into dude ranching because cattle got so cheap he couldn't afford to make a living. We sold calves on the hoof for 3 cents a pound and felt lucky to dispose of them. About that same time they started building feed lots and a rancher could

sell his steers at a reasonable price and they'd take them to a feed lot and fatten them. Ranch beef just went out of style."

Fiesta

Tourists getting a little taste of the cowboy and Mexican life, wearing serapes and dining on fairly elegant cuisine at an Arizona dude ranch. Long-time Tucson resident Marjorie Manning recalls of attending a fiesta in the 1920s. "They had...food that just wouldn't quit. It was just out of this world and . . . of course the main dish was the barbecue. They'd just butcher up the beef and put it in the pit and it would be down there for 24 or

36 hours and when they'd take it out the meat just fell off the bones. One of the most delicious parts of a barbecue is the cow's head. They barbecued the head and everything."

Michelle B. Graye

Apache wickiup
The Western Apaches lived along the mountain ranges in southeastern Arizona during the 1880s, although many Apaches settled in Tucson in earlier centuries. Native Americans living in the Arizona desert learned to make the best of living

arrangements with the building materials available to them, which meant no teepees or wigwams for these Southwest Indians.

Grain storage basket
The Tohono O'odham are superb basket weavers and produce more basketry today than all the other Arizona tribes combined. This huge basket shown in the postcard was intended to hold grain but could serve a dual purpose as a great hid-

ing place for a child to protect him against kidnapping by an agent of the Bureau of Indian Affairs which liked to place Indian children in BIA schools.

Papago pottery

This very colorful card shows a Tohono O'odham woman making pottery, one of the tribe's chief trades, which is mainly done by women. The Spanish, when they began inhabiting the region, called the natives *Papagos*, which means "bean-eaters," a reference to the tribe's main food staple. The name was used until 1986, when the tribe adopted its current constitution and changed back to their original name: Tohono O'odham ("desert people").

Papago girl carrying water

When a young Tohono O'odham girl approached puberty, she would be sent away for four days to an older woman's hut, where she was given guidance by the more worldly woman on how to be a good wife. The young girl would learn the fine art of carrying water and wood which were to be her primary "wifely" duties to make her future husband happy. Returning home from her special training, the girl was given a ceremony recognizing her passage into womanhood. The special carrier used to hold the *olla* or water is called a "burden basket"—well chosen words that perfectly depict the back-breaking chore of carrying water.

45

INDIAN WOMAN GATHERING
SAGUARO CACTUS FRUIT
X 303

Harvesting Saguaro Fruit

The Tohono O'odham women are expert at harvesting saguaro fruit. Using a long L-shaped pole made from mesquite and saguaro ribs, the women would knock the plum-sized fruit off the saguaro. The fruit, which tastes like a raspberry-flavored fig, is then cooked with the seeds strained out to make candy, jelly, and syrup. The syrup can be fermented into a wine for a special ceremony to bring on the summer rains.

Taka

Taka, or toka, is a Tohono O'odham game like field hockey that is played only by women. A team is made up of eleven members, with each player using a long stick, called an usaga, to hit a puck into the other team's goal. The game ends

Papago Women Playing Taka at Rodeo

CHUCK ABBOTT PHOTO

when one side scores but with no set time schedule the game could continue for a long time; the match is usually the best of seven games. For many years the O'odham stopped playing this game that originated centuries ago, but starting in the late 1970s, teenage girls started playing toka again to reconnect with their tribal heritage as well as to get some much needed exercise.

Pagago woman making pottery

The Tohono O'odham is well known for pottery and basketry. Traditionally their pottery always serves a function, and the water pot, or olla, is one of the most important vessels. The typical water jar is three feet high, made out of a very coarse clay that lets the water breathe and keeps it cool through an evaporative process.

PAGO INDIAN MAKING POTTERY, SOUTHERN ARIZONA.

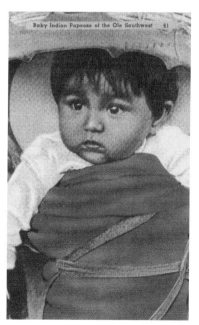

Baby on cradleboard

At one time, the typical Tohono O'odham baby would spend the first year of his life tied to a cradleboard. This allowed the young mother to take the baby along with her as she gathered up firewood and water. The cradleboard could be propped up against the tree or even placed on a sturdy tree limb while she was working, and once she finished her gathering chores, she could just place the baby with cradleboard on top of her load and head back to her tribe.

Michelle B. Graye

Chief Nino Cochise

The man shown on this on this postcard claimed at various times to be the son and even grandson of Chief Cochise, one of the great Chiricahua Apaches. Chief Nino Cochise, as he called himself, made his livelihood by selling his autograph to naive tourists who stopped at his roadside wickiup near Old Tucson.

Indian portrait

Native American postcards were steady sellers and they seem to run in two veins, either really well done photography with a cultural sensitivity toward their subjects or cartoon cards playing to the most blatant stereotypes imagined. Postcard photographers of that era would often travel with costumes and stage photos, so it's not unusual to see the same outfit on different tribe members popping up on postcards.

Out in the Great Open Spaces

Often the postcard vision of what the West was like was based on Hollywood movies or western pulp novels. The Native American standing in his full regalia, including a war bonnet, is wearing the traditional dress of a Plains Indian, not an Indian living in the Southwest. The postcard showing Native Americans pointing at the great open spacious sky in the West is an appealing image the tourists would lap right up and mail to their friends back home, who are eager for pictures of the magnificent "red man" encountered on vacation.

Cartoon postcard of cowgirls

Now don't shoot me for including this postcard; I'm just the messenger here. Forgiving the artist for placing a Southwest Indian in an incorrect headdress, this postcard is more than a wee bit on the offensive side. These cowgirls just seem way too giddy driving home with their prize souvenir strapped on the car hood.

49

Six
NATURE CALLS

The uninformed first-time visitor often has a misconception of what a desert looks like, probably formed from watching movies that show deserts as a barren wasteland. The Sonoran Desert is an arid region whose dominant feature is very little precipitation, but a desert doesn't mean desolation, and the variety of plants and animals that live and thrive in the desert, from cactus to jackrabbit, are a testament to the hardy nature of these specimens – even mosquitoes have found a way to live in Tucson.

Various Species of Cactus as seen on the Desert

Species of cactus
This postcard doubles as an identification guide to the most common species of cactus that exist in the desert. The spelling of "sahuaro" is not the preferred spelling, but tourists have the hardest time pronouncing "saguaro," so a little phonetic help was maybe the intention. Very unlikely the cacti shown here would all be lined up together in one big happy family portrait, can you say cheesy!

Desert Lily

The desert lily bears a bit of a resemblance to the Easter lily and is seen in large numbers growing along desert roads in the springtime. The early settlers called the desert lily "ajo" which means garlic in Spanish, because of the pungent flavor of the bulb. These bulbs will remain underground for several years, waiting for enough rain to emerge in the early spring.

A DESERT LILY

© C. T. CO.

Smoke Tree

This desert scenery postcard with a sunset background really is as gorgeous as pictured. The smoke tree featured in this card has a plume-like growth and a golden color that give the tree a smoky appearance, hence its name. The trunk is small and crooked, with a grayish-brown bark that is scaly. The tree will branch out and grow to a height of twenty feet when mature.

SMOKE TREE ON THE DESERT

Ocotillo

The ocotillo (oak-oh-tee-yo) is often referred to as the monkey tail cactus. It is not actually a cactus but a shrub. The plant is made of spindly stems that are 10 to 15 feet long, joined at the base, then fanned out, whip-like and straight,

OCOTILLO IN BLOOM ON THE DESFRT

angling outward like a peacock's tail. The ocotillo can be used to make a living fence, and Native Americans suck the nectar out of the buds and also use this nectar to make tea.

Prickly Pear

Probably one of the most recognizable cacti in the Southwest, these colorful beauties are easily grown and have distinctive flattened pads, each of which can

be rooted to form a new plant. These cacti store water in their stems, plumping out when it rains and looking shriveled up during periods of drought. The tiny, bristly spines are pretty sharp and have quite a bite to them when you handle or accidentally brush into them. Their rose-pink flowers bloom in spring, and the fruit of the prickly pear can be used to make soups, jelly, and even a refreshing juice if you harvest enough of the fruit.

52

Desert silhouette

The best time to view some of nature's spectacular handiwork is really early in the morning or after the sun sets. Next to the San Xavier Mission, the postcards that depict wildlife and the saguaro cactus dominate rack space at the gift racks. *Arizona Highways* has become one of the premiere magazines because they know the power of the pretty desert scenery.

Saguaro cactus

The saguaro (pronounced sah-whar-oh) is found naturally growing only in the Sonoran Desert, the only place on the planet where these cacti are native. They do not begin to bloom with the distinctive fragrant white and yellow flowers until age 60 (their life span is up to 200 years). The Tucson area used to have bragging rights to the world's tallest cactus, but in 2003 a new champ standing tall at 46 feet was located in the Tonto Forest north of Scottsdale. A Tucson newspaper took it pretty hard and ran an article urging the local citizenry to go out immediately and hunt down an even taller green giant to reclaim the title.

53

Night-blooming cereus

The night blooming cereus is a member of the cactus family, and most of its life goes unnoticed because it resembles dead sticks leaning on other desert shrubs.

But on one glorious night in late June or early July, the plant unveils its beauty, opening as night falls and releasing a sweet scent to attract moths and other nocturnal pollinators. Once the morning comes, the flower closes up shop forever.

Spanish Bayonet

This extremely striking plant, also commonly known as Our Lord's Candle, is a species of yucca found in the Arizona desert and parts of Southern California. This yucca plant has a tall woody stem, stiff sword-like pointed leaves, and clusters of white flowers. The young flower stalk is roasted and eaten by Native Americans. The yucca fibers can also be used as a common material in Indian baskets.

Coyote

The coyote, also referred to as the "song dog" by many Native Americans, is an extremely intelligent animal that has learned to survive by living near the urban fringes of what used to be their habitat. The coyote lives by

scavenging food and is well-adapted to eating everything it can wolf down, including jackrabbits, beetles, mice, grapes, melons, and even leftover fast food foraged from construction sites. Though they look like your average house dog, coyotes are not tame and can be brutal killers, especially to the cat and poodle population in Tucson.

Javelina

The collared peccary or javelina (pronounced have-a-leen-a) got its name from the Spanish word javelin, or sword, in reference to their tusks. Javelinas aren't actually pigs but do share a similar appearance. The javelina is a magnificent animal standing in at about 3 feet tall and weighing almost 60 pounds when fully grown. Though the *javelina* may appear cute and cuddly, many homeowners have horror stories to recount about a pet or family member being attacked by an agitated javelina mother protecting her young. They eat mostly fruits, vegetables, insects, and even cactus pads.

Michelle B. Graye

Gambel's Quail

These plump birds with the distinguished teardrop-shaped plume live in groups of up to 200 during the winter. Since they aren't such great fliers they live mostly on the ground. Their feathers are rich in colors of chestnut, cream, gray, and

[reprinted with permission] ©TheLaughin' Place

brown that blend in nicely with the desert to help conceal them from the predators flying above. The quail's favorite foods include leaves, shoots, new green vegetation, and insects. Quite talkative, these birds can really make a racket when startled, squawking with a variety of clucks and whistles and running around in all directions to distract their would-be predators.

Roadrunner

ARIZONA ROADRUNNER

The roadrunner, true to its name, prefers to run rather than fly. The long legs are really an advantage when chasing down prey of mice, insects, and scorpions, which are usually no match for the bird's swiftness. Though the roadrunner is New Mexico's state bird, Arizona has its fair share of these clownish-looking birds that show up in the oddest places, even running into buildings if an opportunity presents itself.

Gila Monster

The gila (pronounced HEE-lah) monster, purportedly the only venomous lizard in the United States, lives most of its life in a burrow, hibernating for long periods of time. The gila monster's favorite food is quail eggs, but also has an appetite for young rabbits and squirrels. This magnificent creature measures between one and two feet long at adulthood. Despite a fierce appearance, the gila is a shy and

gentle creature unless provoked—then watch out. The bite is more painful than a rattlesnake's. No anti-venin is available if you are bitten, and though a bite might not kill you, be prepared to feel nauseated and weak.

Horned Toad

The horned toad likes to bask in the sun's rays a few hours every day until its body temperature rises to a specific degree, and once that occurs this little guy starts foraging for food. A voracious eater, the horned toad can consume up to one hundred ants in a day. Other favorite foods include spiders, ticks, moth larvae and even butterflies.

Rattlesnake

Eleven species of rattlesnakes live in the Southwest region, and though bites

from them are rare, they will strike out and bite. Rattlers have broad heads and wide, gaping articulated jaws that can unhinge to swallow creatures much larger then you can imagine. Swallowing a whole rabbit seems like a contortionist's trick. With the ability to unhinge his jaw to 180 degrees, the rattlesnake might not have the best table manners but he's an effective eating machine. The rattlesnake bite is dangerous but usually not lethal.

Buzzard

Mother Nature must have been in one foul mood when she designed this desert scavenger. Buzzards, or turkey vultures, are large, powerfully-built birds with inadequate leg strength to carry live prey, so they work in conjunction with the

sun which rots and putrefies dead animals, a perfect feast for the vulture, who is immune to bacteria and toxins. Vultures will eat to the point of gluttony, and if threatened, they'll spew their guts as an effective defense mechanism.

Tucson Mountain Park

Created in 1930, Tucson Mountain Park borders the Saguaro National Park and encompasses 20,000 acres to preserve the habitat of the desert wildlife. Besides having the opportunity of seeing the desert in its natural state, visitors coming to Tucson Mountain Park can participate in lots of other activities, including hiking, horseback riding, and picnicking.

Tinted Road

This rather striking hand-tinted card shows how saguaros can grow to dramatically different heights. Though they have an imposing sturdy appearance and impressive spines, saguaros are actually quite fragile. Many potential dangers stand in the way of their living up to 200 years of age. Loss of limbs from harsh winds, being struck by lightning, prolonged exposure to freezing temperatures, and even tiny bacteria that can invade holes bored by woodpeckers can all lead to an early death for this silent sentinel. Don't be fooled by the unpaved road in this postcard; Tucson has very few of these left, and saguaros do suffer from car exhaust just like the rest of us.

59

Seven
SCHOOL DAYS:
THE UNIVERSITY OF ARIZONA

Bird's-eye view of campus

In 1885, when Arizona was still a territorial government, the legislature decided to divvy up the plums among the major cities. Up for grabs was the capitol, a college, and an insane asylum. The good folks of Tucson had their hearts set on nab-

bing the insane asylum, but their delegate arrived late to Prescott and was given the left-over booby prize: the university. Upon returning to Tucson with the bad news, the poor delegate was reportedly greeted by jeers and pelted with rotten eggs, vegetables, and even a dead cat. The citizens soon got over their disappointment and, with $25,000 appropriated by the territorial legislature and a 40-acre tract of land donated by two gamblers and a saloon keeper, the University of Arizona was born

Campus scene

This postcard shows the park and library, which was built in 1904 as a library and museum. Over the years it has housed various colleges and departments, including the college of law. Campus life back then was very different. The students

would ride their horses to class and tie them to hitching posts near Old Main. Students were expected to be on their best behavior, and demerits would be handed out for all types of infractions, including running on the balcony of Old Main (you would be slapped with ten demerits for that one).

Main Gate

In 1905 the main gate, which was made of barbed wire fencing and featured a wooden turnstile, was revamped with brick pillars and a low stone wall. Up until this time a horse and mule-drawn trolley served the campus from downtown; this

MAIN GATE UNIVERSITY OF ARIZONA. TUCSON.

was replaced by the newfangled electric trolley. Further changes to the main gate occurred in 1916, when the low stone wall was upgraded with a lava rock wall that continues to mark where the University of Arizona campus originated.

View from West Main Gate

This view shows the original Old Main building, just inside the west main gate

on campus. The date palm trees lining the street give a sweeping majestic look to the campus, which at one time had only one building and two schools (Mines and Engineering). The campus has always had a reputation for being one of the prettiest around. Some famous name attendees that have graced the campus include Morris K. Udall, Linda McCartney, Geraldo Rivera, Don Knotts, Greg Kinnear, Garry Shandling, Linda Ronstadt, Ted De Grazia, Bob Dole, Annika Sorenstam, Sean Elliott, J.A. Jance, and Barry Goldwater.

Michelle B. Graye

Liberal Arts and Humanities Buildings

This typical campus scene shows the liberal arts and humanities buildings in

1943. The time of year is probably mid-winter, when the balmy weather allows for shirt sleeves and lounging outside. The date palms, evergreens, and olive trees all flourish during the mild winter months.

Old Main

The University of Arizona officially opened its doors on October 1, 1891. Six professors and thirty-two students were crammed into a single building now known as Old Main. The downstairs was used for classrooms, library, living quarters for the professors, and offices. The students lived on the second floor.

The first graduating class of 1895 had three people. The building was condemned at one time, but it got a second life when the government used it as a naval training school during World War II, when it had an ongoing class of 500 men.

Mines and Engineering Building

Mines and agriculture were the first two colleges, holding classes in the university's only building, Old Main. There were sixteen students in the freshman class of 1892. Only one member of this class, Mrs. Clara Fish, was eligible to graduate in 1896. University officials refused to put on graduation exercises for only one student and forced her to complete another year of school, graduating her with the class of 1897.

271. MINES AND ENGINEERING BUILDING, UNIVERSITY OF ARIZONA, TUCSON, ARIZONA. 121413

University of Arizona Fountain

This eye-pleasing fountain was built in 1919, at the west entrance of Old Main, to honor the University of Arizona students who lost their lives during World War I. The money to build the fountain was donated by Alexander Berger, an uncle of one of the fallen students. At the dedication of the fountain, General "Black Jack" Pershing gave a speech, impressive in its content as well as brevity. The fountain also serves as a wishing well, with coins being tossed by students and faculty hoping for good fortune to come their way.

Michelle B. Graye

Cheerleaders making U of A formation

The University of Arizona has always loved its sports teams, as evidenced by this cheerleading formation, showing off the vibrant school colors of cardinal red and

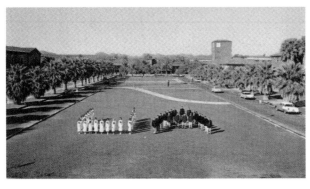

navy blue. It's a source of school pride to wear as much red as possible on game days, and Wildcat fans are legion in promoting school spirit. The U of A's original colors were sage green and silver, but frugal-minded student manager Quintas J. Anderson was offered a bargain deal on some jerseys in 1900 that were solid blue and trimmed in red, so he bought the team some new jerseys and the new school colors were enthusiastically received and approved.

Football Stadium

This more modern view of the University of Arizona showcases the football stadium, which has served as the home for the football team since 1929. The seating capacity in those days was a paltry 7,000 but with expansions the stadium can

hold almost 58,000 Wildcat fans. The stadium also addresses a pressing need at most universities, a shortage of dorm space. Four floors of dorm rooms, some of them quite spacious are part of the stadium, following the curve of the football stadium. Students living in these dorms have stated the noise level (which can be quite raucous during football games) is only minimal due to the thick concrete block-wall construction.

Eight
TOURIST TRAPPINGS

La Fiesta de los Vaqueros

It was in the 1920s that Tucson first started marketing the city a place where tourists would want to visit. The Tucson Sunshine Climate Club was specifically formed to promote the fabulous weather and the rugged natural beauty of the desert. The rodeo is a huge event for which schools, including the University of Arizona, declare a holiday, Rodeo Day. All students are given the day off to attend the event. The founders of the rodeo envisioned it to someday be as famous as Mardi Gras and the Miss America Beauty Pageant.

Before the rodeo, Tucson puts on the largest non-motorized parade in the world, an annual event since 1925. The Rodeo Day Parade is one of the most well-loved events in the city's winter season and is a perennial magnet for snowbirds visiting Tucson from all parts of the globe.

Michelle B. Graye

Desert Museum entrance

The non-profit Arizona- Sonora Desert Museum is a world class living natural history museum located west of town on the same land as Tucson Mountain Park.

Started in 1952, the Desert Museum gets bragging rights to the second most popular attraction for visitors to Arizona after the Grand Canyon. One of the most popular animals during the museum's early days was a mountain lion named George L. Mountainlion. George was such a big star he even wrote (with a little human help) a weekly column for the *Arizona Daily Star.*

Desert Museum tunnel entrance

The museum prides itself on offering visitors an opportunity to view the desert

animals in as close to their natural habitat as possible. The Desert Museum tunnel was built in 1957 and was unique for the time, allowing visitors to go underground and see how the animals lived during the daytime.

San Xavier Mission

A newspaper reporter humorously reported the San Xavier Mission as "the church that launched a thousand Tucson postcards" and anyone driving on the freeway can't miss this majestic mission rising out of the desert. Best known as the "White Dove of the Desert," San Xavier del Bac was established on a site first visited in 1692 by Father Eusebio Francisco Kino. Padre Kino never got around to the building of a church; this task fell to the Franciscan priests who took fourteen years to complete the mammoth con-

San Xavier Mission, Tucson, Ariz.

struction project (1783-1797). The unfinished tower is a source of great speculation and various stories range from a worker falling off the tower and getting killed, leaving superstitious workers to spooked to finish their work, or possibly frugal-minded missionaries leaving the tower uncompleted because, once finished taxes, would have to be paid back to the Spanish Crown.

San Xavier Mission with Papago women in the foreground

The San Xavier Mission is still run by the Franciscans which serve the Tohono O'odham community of Bac (which loosely translated means "place where the water appears"). The mission plays an important part in the lives of the Tohono O'odham people who set up stands to sell their handicrafts and delicious fare of honey popovers and tortillas to visiting tourists. The church is open daily to visitors with special masses being held for the interested worshipper.

San Xavier Mission, from Papago Indian Settlement, Arizona

San Xavier Mission view from the east

From any angle, the mission is a feast for the eyes. The mission remains one of

the finest examples of Spanish Colonial architecture in the United States. The multiple buildings shown in the post-card served a variety of purposes, including a school, meeting rooms and gift shop.

San Xavier Mission interior view

The interior of the church is just as beautiful as the outside, and visitors are encouraged to buy special candles in the gift shop to leave as an offering at altars. The walls are decorated with elaborate murals and carvings depicting stories from the Bible and the history of Christianity. The soot from the burning candles has dulled the murals over the last hundred years but an extensive restoration by skilled craftsmen has really restored the vibrant colors of the interior.

Old Tucson Stage Depot

Visitors flocking to Tucson are delighted to visit the Old Tucson Studios, a site for the making of over 200 films and television series. Originally Old Tucson built as a stage set for the 1939 film *Arizona* which starred Jean Arthur and William Holden. Much care and expense went into building this set, an impressive recreation of how Tucson might have looked in the 1860s.

Main Street looking south - Old Tucson - Tucson Mtn. Park - Tucson, Ariz.

Old Tucson overview

After the filming of *Arizona* the buildings were left to gather dust with no clear function except for the visitors that liked to traipse around the dormant set. The movie industry saw a resurgence of Westerns in the 1950s and Old Tucson found new life as some great Westerns were filmed there, including *Gunfight at the OK Corral, Winchester '73,* and *Rio Bravo.* John Wayne loved coming to Old Tucson so much he even bought stock in the Old Tucson Development Company.

Michelle B. Graye

Old Tucson Main Street

The movie stars that have walked this street over the years are a virtual who's who of Hollywood. Following is a partial list:

Gene Autry, Ingrid Bergman, Marlon Brando, Gary Cooper, Bing Crosby, Tony Curtis, Marlene Dietrich, Kirk Douglas, Clark Gable, Clint Eastwood, Rock Hudson, Burt Lancaster, Michael Landon, Jack Lemmon, Sophia Loren, Dean Martin, Lee Marvin, Robert Mitchum, Paul Newman, Maureen O'Hara, Gregory Peck, Sidney Poitier, Anthony Quinn, Ronald Reagan, Barbara Stanwyck, Jimmy Stewart, Spencer Tracy, John Wayne and Joanne Woodward.

Shoot-Out at Old Tucson

The highlight of any visit to Old Tucson has to be witnessing the gunfights between the well-trained stuntmen. These actors have to undergo extensive training to be able to fall off buildings and participate convincingly in old fashioned shoot-em-ups. Over the years Old Tucson became concerned about glorifying violence so the actors are only wounded and don't really die.

70

Kitt Peak National Observatory

Located almost sixty miles west of town, Kitt Peak has the world's largest collection of optical telescopes. Located on land leased to the federal government by the Tohono O'odham people, the site was chosen over 150 other mountain peaks screened by a committee of astronomers between 1955–1958. The night stargazing viewing programs are very popular. Visitors leaving for the evening get an added adventure of a hair-raising trip down the mountain with just

your parking lights on. Car lights are not allowed to be turned on because they disturb the work of the big telescopes in action.

Flandrau Planetarium

Flandrau Planetarium (opened December 13, 1975), is located on the University of Arizona campus and was constructed with $800,000 donated by Mrs. Grace H. Flandrau. The Pima County Supervisors wanted to build a snazzy million-dollar planetarium in 1969 to honor Frank Borman, a local boy who made good as commander of the Apollo 8 space mission, but the voters rejected the proposal. With the money donated by Mrs. Flandrau, the facility was world class all the way and featured the use of an innovative fish-eye lens combined with

a projection system that covers a 360-degree area, making for an eye-popping, dazzling display in the dome theater.

71

Colossal Cave Bandit's Hold

Colossal Cave was formed millions of years ago by the welling up of hot sulfur brine It is the largest dormant or dry cave in the United States and, though offi-

cially discovered in 1879, the cave has been used for centuries by local tribes for shelter and storage. The various formations and areas are given really creative nicknames including Kingdom of the Elves, Witches' Den, Elvis and Bandit's Hold. According to old-timers, a group of train robbers took cover with their loot in this cave in the 1800s. The Tucson sheriff tried to starve them out but, once entering the cave, never did find these outlaws, who had already skeedaddled to a saloon in another town where they were heard bragging about their exploits .

Colossal Cave interior

The tour through this cave only covers a half-mile route and, with forty miles mapped, the cave still has not been fully explored. Being a dry or dormant cave allows for some amazing formations of stalactites, stalagmites, and flowstone. The temperature in the cave is always around a refreshing 70 to 71 degrees year around.

72

Hi Corbett Field

Tucson Baseball Commissioner Hiram "Hi" Corbett was a man with a vision when, in 1945, he was able to persuade legendary baseball owner Bill Veeck to bring spring training to Tucson. The base-ball field built for a little over $32,000 was originally called Randolph Field and served as the winter home for the Cleveland Indians. Lots of sunshine, baseball and beer make for an enjoy-able afternoon at the ballpark, bringing in much-needed tourist dollars for the city.

Greyhound Park

Before there were Indian gaming casinos, lotteries and Las Vegas, Tucson had Greyhound Park, one of the oldest gambling establishments in Arizona, having been in business since 1944. Located in South Tucson, the park would run for only 2 months of the year, in accor-dance with the law that would put a limit on year around gambling. Greyhound Park is now open year around and even offers up off-track betting to help keep it competitive with the gaming casinos.

Pima Air Museum

Opened to the public in 1976 as Pima Air Museum, Pima Air & Space Museum is now the largest privately funded aerospace museum in the world. Originally

the museum was a WWII barracks but it now offers up exhibits of more than 250 aircraft from pre-World War I to the present. Some of the more noteworthy planes on exhibit include the tiny Bumble Bee, the world's smallest piloted airplane, and Air Force One used by both John F. Kennedy and Lyndon Baines Johnson.

Davis-Monthan AFB (AMARC)

Tucson Municipal Airport (originally constructed in 1919) was later moved east of the Southern Pacific Railroad tracks and renamed Davis-Monthan, after two Tucson World War I pilots who lost their lives in the line of duty. Charles Lindbergh flew in fresh from his world record breaking nonstop crossing of the Atlantic to handle dedication duties in 1927. The dry baked earth makes the Aerospace Maintenance and Regeneration Center (AMARC), or Desert Boneyard, the ideal place for planes to sit in outdoor storage until it's time to salvage them for surplus.

Mount Lemmon Highway

The Mount Lemmon Highway, or Hitchcock Highway, was started in 1933 as a Federal Prison Corps program to put inmates and illegal immigrants to work during the hard eco-nomic times of the Great Depression. Even though the work was back-breaking, the jobs were very desirable because they offer-ed a chance to be outdoors. The road up to Mount Lem-mon was completed and dedicated in 1948. The distance

from the base of the mountain to the top on the paved road is 29 miles. When the road was being built, the government only allowed visitors to drive the complet-ed section of the road on Sundays.

Mount Lemmon Store and Inn

When the locals grow fatigued from the never-ending sunshine and triple digit daily temperatures, they know relief is only an hour away on Mount Lemmon. There can be a change of 30 degrees from the city basin to the top of Mount Lemmon and snow-fall is not that unusual in the win-tertime though it melts pretty quick-ly. An immense forest fire on Mount Lemmon in 2003 destroyed most of the cabins and caused millions of dollars of losses in property damage.

MT. LEMMON

STORE & INN

Mt. Lemmon,

Arizona

near Tucson

A-177

Michelle B. Graye

Sabino Canyon

Any area that offers a cool oasis and even running springs is revered by Tucsonans and over a million visitors a year make their way to Sabino Canyon. Located in the Santa Catalinas, the canyon is a nature lover's dream spot. Sabino

Canyon offers many attractions including desert wildflowers and animals, hiking, recreational trails, waterfalls, and rugged rock formations. A tram staffed by knowledgeable volunteers is a fun way to see this beautiful, easily accessible desert sanctuary.

Seven Falls

Located in Bear Canyon, Seven Falls is worth the four-mile hike through some

of the prettiest views offered in the desert. The waterfalls can be quite dangerous depending on the time of year, and the newspaper runs at least one story every few years of a hiker falling to his death while navigating the slippery waterfalls. The water is always ice cold

from the runoff from the snowfall, so make sure to keep your socks dry when you wade across the pools of water.

Sir George's Royal Buffet

Before the all-you-can-eat buffets were dotting the landscapes of every urban center, Tucson had Sir George's with its throwback medieval decor making it a perfect dinner getaway when facing the hot stove seems like an impossible task. On Sundays this was the  place to take your family after church, still dressed up, to enjoy a nice dinner out. Tucson was graced with two Royal George's and, sadly, both are long gone but not forgotten

Pinnacle Peak

Located in Trail Dust Town, a series of buildings originally designed as a set for a Glenn Ford movie in the 1950s, Pinnacle Peak now anchors the western-themed commercial strip-front. Known for their huge steaks cooked over mesquite coals, prospective diners need be warned about the no-necktie rule. If a customer is caught wearing a tie, be prepared for a waiter to run over to your table, and with much fanfare cut off the offending neckwear and hang it from the rafters. It's a badge of honor to have your tie snipped so make sure to keep your expensive designer  tie at home when eating at Pinnacle Peak.

Michelle B. Graye

El Charro Restaurant

LOCATED IN PRESIDIO HISTORIC DISTRICT

311 NORTH COURT   TUCSON, ARIZONA 85701   602-622-5465

Located in the historic El Presidio district downtown, El Charro wins the honors of being the longest running Mexican restaurant continuously operated by the same family in the United States. El Charro is well known for their carne seca which is seasoned and dried in a special cage located on the premises. El Charro sets the bar for having some of the most delicious fare in Tucson. Monica Flin, daughter of master stonecutter Jules Flin, opened the first El Charro Restaurant out of a modest storefront on 4th Avenue in 1922. Three moves later, the restaurant has been happily ensconced at its present location which was the original Flin family home built in 1896.

El Merendero Restaurant

Located in the St. Philip's Plaza, this very old world Mexico-looking restaurant was built in the 1930s. The architects were very clever in using vintage windows, timber and door frames brought up from Mexico. It's a tough business running a restaurant in Tucson and El Merendero just never caught fire and was eventually sold to the adjacent St. Philip's Church which needed additional space for their parishioners.

Bibliography

Bret Harte, John. *Tucson Portrait of a Desert Pueblo.* 1980. Woodland Hills, CA: Windsor Publications.

Cobb, Vicki. *This Place is Dry!* 1989. New York: Walker.

Cooper, Evelyn S. *The Buehman Studio Tucson in Focus.* 1995. Tucson, AZ: Arizona Historical Society.

Cox, Larry. *The Book of Tucson Firsts.* 1998. Tucson, AZ: Javelina Press.

Dillon, Richard. *Arizona's Amazing Towns: From Wild West to High Tech.* 1992. Tempe, AZ: Four Peaks Press.

Dutton, A.A. *Arizona Then & Now.* 2002. Englewood, CO: Westcliffe Publishers.

Grimes, Paul L. *Tucson Rodeo Parade & Museum: Stories-Memories-Tales Since 1925.* 1991. Tucson, AZ: The Tucson Rodeo Parade Committee.

Farley, Stephen (editor). *Snapped on the Street.* 1999. Tucson, AZ: Tucson Voices Press.

Henry, Bonnie. *Another Tucson.* 1992. Tucson, AZ: Arizona Daily Star.

Kamper, John and Donna. *Tucson Uncovered.* 1996. Plano, TX: Seaside Press.

Kopp, April. *Creatures, Critters & Crawlers of the Southwest.* 1996. Santa Fe, NM: New Mexico Magazine.

Nequette, Anne M. and R. Brooks Jeffries. 2002. *A Guide to Tucson Architecture.* Tucson, AZ: University of Arizona Press.

Sheaffer, Jack. *Jack Sheaffer's Tucson 1945-1965.* 1985. Tucson, AZ: Arizona Daily Star.

Sonnichsen, C.L. *Tucson the Life and Times of an American City.* 1982. Norman, OK: University of Oklahoma Press.

Stephensen, Patricia and Alex Jay Kimmelman. *Tom Marshall's Tucson.* 1996. Tucson, AZ: Patricia Peters Stephenson.

Trimble, Marshall. *Arizona 2000: a Yearbook for the Millennium.* Flagstaff, AZ: Northland Pub.

Tweit, Susan J. *The Great Southwest Nature Factbook.* 1992. Seattle, WA: Alaska Northwest Books.

Underhill, Ruth. *The Papago Indians of Arizona and Their Relatives the Pima.* 1940. Washington, D.C.: Education Division, U.S. Office of Indian Affairs.

INDEX